Luther Brokaw

1941.

CALVARY TO-DAY

OTHER BOOKS BY BISHOP FISKE

Christ and Christianity ("The Christ We Know" and "The Faith By Which We Live" in one volume.)
The Real Jesus (Written in collaboration with Professor Burton Scott Easton.)
The Christ We Know: A Study of the Life of Jesus for the New Generation
The Confessions of a Puzzled Parson
The Faith By Which We Live
The Perils of Respectability
The Experiment of Faith
Sacrifice and Service
Back to Christ

OUT OF PRINT

The Religion of the Incarnation
The Church: What It Is and What It Does

CALVARY TO-DAY

The Words from the Cross
to
Modern Men and Women

BY THE RIGHT REVEREND

CHARLES FISKE

S.T.D., L.H.D., LL.D.

BISHOP OF CENTRAL NEW YORK

MOREHOUSE PUBLISHING CO.
MILWAUKEE, WISCONSIN

First printing, November, 1929
Second printing, February, 1930
Third printing, March, 1930

CONTENTS

WITH HUMILITY AND HESITATION

A Preface and Apology

WITH HUMILITY AND HESITATION

THESE are Good Friday addresses given in Trinity Church, New York City, and published at the suggestion of some hearers who felt that meditations of this type—simple, direct, homely, practical, unpretentious—would be useful on other Good Fridays for pastors and people of other congregations.

I hesitate to print them, because, for the life of me, I cannot remember what thoughts are my own and what have been culled from others. Each Good Friday, for many years, I have prepared long before for the Three Hours of Devotion by consulting note books in which I have jotted down thoughts arrived at through reading or original study; then I have given myself to meditation until the addresses took shape and I could come to the pulpit full of the great subject on which I was to preach—at least full of the spirit of the day, if not full of novel or original ideas.

The addresses are given as they were delivered, with no possibility of acknowledging sources from which ideas may have come. I hesitate to print such informal meditations, and only the kindly enthusiasm of members of the congregation who heard them has overcome the hesitation.

Even with such requests pushing me on, I feel doubtful. After all, was it the preacher or the congregation that gave the words wings? Anyone who has ever attended a Good Friday service at Old Trinity, seeing the crowded church with hundreds packed into every available space, filling the chancel, crowded to the altar rail, sitting on the pulpit steps, standing, some far out of sight in a distant chapel, other hundreds stretching out in massed lines through the vestibules into the old graveyard and far over toward the street, with "loud speakers" to carry the words to those who cannot see, and knowing (in some years) that countless others were "listening in" over the radio—

anyone whose good fortune it has been to attend such a service will know that the preacher counts for very little; it is the congregation that counts by helping him to pour into the poorest of sermons all the faith and love he longs to impart. It is not the thought of the preacher that matters; it is the indescribable something which the preacher catches from the faces of a congregation hungry for the great truths of the day. If some who heard these addresses find them disappointing in print, let them remember that these pages simply sketch the outline of what they preached to themselves, to which the speaker merely gave imperfect voice as their mouthpiece. C. F.

INTRODUCTORY ADDRESS

Companions of the Saviour

"And when they were come to the place, which is called Calvary, there they crucified Him, and the malefactors, one on the right hand, and the other on the left." St. Luke XXIII: 33.

COMPANIONS OF THE SAVIOUR

WE MEET here, on this Good Friday, as Companions of the Saviour. And we know He wants us to come. It is touching, as we read the story of His passion, to learn how He longed for the presence and sympathy of His friends. Jesus Christ is as perfectly human as He is truly divine. He came to reveal the Friendly God, who entered into the tragedy of human life to show that He understands and sympathizes and helps and saves. Because Jesus is human as well as divine, He not only *gave* friendship, He *needed* friends. There is something pathetically human in His longing for their friendship and love. "What! Could ye not watch with Me one brief hour?" There is something sweetly human in His appreciation of their loyalty and love. "Ye are they which have *continued with Me* in My temptation."

In the deepest experiences of life we often

wish to be alone; yet companionship, if it be of the right sort, is always appreciated. The friend who is satisfied just to be with us—not to talk, but just to be with us, if we feel that *we* must speak—one whose presence helps and strengthens: we all know what such a friend means in the hour of trial. In His most sacred hour Jesus wanted His friends to be near.

So we are here as companions of the suffering Saviour. Our presence shows that we care. And, please God, we shall depart, when the Three Hours of Devotion are ended, not to go away from Him and forget, but to keep Him always as our Companion. We wish to make this Good Friday a new experience of friendship with Him—a friendship in His sorrows which will pass into the friendship of service.

All this may seem to you a bit of sentimental mysticism; so I must preface the meditations today with a few words of homely counsel.

Three things I want you to remember. First, do not expect anything new or novel.

Second, even in the thought of companionship with Christ, do not try to strain after the emotional; be natural; be silent, quiet, thoughtful. Finally, try during the addresses and in your devotions to realize the full meaning of Calvary.

Do not expect anything new. I have been preaching the passion every Good Friday for more than thirty years. One who tells year by year this Old, Old Story is apt to feel that in some way he must give it a touch of novelty. The Good Friday preacher thinks of the Words from the Cross as pearls of wisdom, truth, and love; and then there is the probability that he will be over-anxious to find a new thread on which to string the pearls—some central thought running through them all by which he may give a continuous message. The danger is, that in the effort to bend the Seven Words to the central thought, he may become unnatural, forced, unreal, artificial.

Today we shall take the Words in their natural, unforced meaning. That meaning is always the same. The application may be different; the message may strike a new note; special circumstances may give the message its special significance. But that is quite as much your work as mine. I shall leave you to preach each address over again in your own hearts, as you kneel in the silence. So there will be no strain of artificiality in the addresses. They will attempt to make you see vividly each scene. But there will be nothing new.

Again, do not strain after emotional effect. We are false to the sacred solemnity of the service, if we do that; there will be a touch of insincerity in our meditations. For this is Good Friday—not that Friday of the Crucifixion, when the lookers-on at Calvary were in the depths of defeat, the heavens as brass over their heads, the earth reeling under their feet. We know that the Friday of death was followed by the Easter of victorious life. We can never forget this. It would be a piece of dramatic legerdemain if we tried to forget it. We shall think of the events of Good Friday, but we shall think of them, quietly, in the light of what followed Good Friday. The chief thing is to center our thoughts on the lessons we learn, in the confidence of that certain faith which makes the Words of the Sufferer sure messages from the heart of the Eternal God.

That brings me to my third suggestion. In genuineness and sincerity, try to see what today's story really means in the light of what follows Good Friday. The story is not merely about Jesus. It is about God. There may be many here today who do not quite believe this. We are glad they are here. Only, if Good Friday is nothing more than the commemoration of the world's worst tragedy, it cannot bring much of hope or peace. It only shows us the Best Man that ever lived, apparently deserted by God at the end and paying the price of a foolish idealism.

That is not what Christ's first companions believed in the light of their later experiences, and it is for this reason I ask you not to place yourselves in their position at the Cross, but to look at the passion through the clear atmosphere of their later knowledge, when they had discovered that their eyes had gazed upon the Word of Life and that they had seen the light of the knowledge of the glory of God in the face of Jesus Christ.

These first disciples believed that the Cross of Calvary showed them what God is. The Gospels are transparently honest in telling the story in the language of their first experience and without minimizing their first despondency and despair. To realize how honest they were, you must remember how frank the Gospels are in the disclosure of the weakness and cowardice of the disciples; you must remember that they dared to tell of the treachery of one of their number, that they were never afraid to record how they all forsook their Leader and fled, that they hid nothing of the foolish boasting of St. Peter and his subsequent denial, that they put down, without equivocation or evasion, all the story of their unbelief and their slow and faltering return to faith, that they left in their memoirs of the passion one word from the Cross which seemed to show their Master's loss of faith and trust when He felt utterly forsaken in His desolation.

Yes, they were honest—these writers of

the Gospels; so honest that in the primitive Gospel record the one dying word of their Master left in the story is that unexplained cry: "My God, My God, why hast Thou forsaken Me?" They were just as honest in their belief that the Cross of Christ showed them what God is. All that Jesus was, God is; all that He did, God does; all that He said, God says; all that He felt, in the infinite affection of His infinitely loving heart, God feels.

That is what the earliest companions of Jesus came to believe. And it changed them. If you see one who seems to you to be the most lovable person you know suffering, because of what you have done, it will change you. And when you discover what your indifference or sin means to God, that will change you. Sin will no longer be lightly passed over as a foolish mistake or an unfortunate slip. Certainly you will discover it to be something more than a psychological reaction in the stuff of your material make-up.

Sometimes it is hard to hold our faith in a *personal* God. For myself, I have found that the only sure ground of such a faith lies in belief in the Incarnate Son. It is harder yet to believe in a *loving* God, and there, assuredly, your only sure standing ground is belief in an Incarnate Saviour, whose life is the unveiling of the heart of Deity. We begin the devotions with a prayer that this faith may be strengthened in all of us as we meditate on the story which tells how God was in Christ reconciling the world to Himself. And we pray that for today at least our penitence may so cleanse our hearts that we may know God's love and hold fast our faith in Him despite all doubt and difficulty.

THE FIRST WORD

The Prayer of Forgiveness

"Father, forgive them; for they know not what they do." St. Luke XXIII: 34.

THE PRAYER OF FORGIVENESS

WHAT Christ was, God is. We think of God as almighty—which means, for most of us, that we think He can do whatever He chooses to do. The fact is, that God is love; and God can do only what love can do.

Love in the end is unconquerable. You may crucify it, but it will rise again. God can do only what love can do; but love can go on loving all the time, even when it is hurt most. Yes, it keeps on loving all the time; in the correct translation, the first word from the Cross bears this introductory phrase, not "Jesus *said,* 'Father, forgive them' "; but, "Jesus *kept on saying,* 'Father, forgive them.' " As if He said it, and then said it again, and then again and again.

Picture the scene. It is a place of public execution, with a dense crowd of people pressing close to the victim—a scene not unlike a public hanging a generation or two ago. It is holiday time and the city is thronged with people who have come up for the Passover festivities. Their one topic of conversation had been the validity of the claims of this alleged Messiah, or Priest-King. Jesus was suffering execution because these claims on His part had been rejected by the rulers of Israel. Priests, Pharisees, Scribes would have accepted Him, had He been willing to be a Messiah after their own heart. But His teaching was too high and lofty for them and they fought Him to the death—fought Him even to the point of denial of their national ambitions. "Shall I crucify your king?" And they answered, "We have no king but Caesar."

He had been betrayed by the priests and rulers. He was betrayed by Pilate, from whom He might have expected the traditional Roman justice. He was betrayed by the people—and that was hardest of all. He did not fit in with the popular idea of a Messiah. They looked for a leader who would make headway against the power of

Rome, and overthrow the foreign yoke, and restore the kingdom to Israel; but He preached peace and goodwill, and talked of a spiritual kingdom for which they then had no desire. So they turned on Him in chagrin. He forfeited their allegiance, and at the instigation of their leaders they raised a hue and cry against Him.

Now Jesus is paying the penalty of His foolish idealism. We cannot appreciate the wonder of this prayer of forgiveness, unless we see the scene as it was, with that holiday crowd mad with excitement, turning on a leader who had disappointed them—a fickle crowd as crazy over a popular rabbi as any American crowd ever went mad over a popular hero, and just as ready as the modern man to banish the hero to oblivion at the first revulsion of feeling.

The trouble with the crowd on Calvary was the same trouble we discover in crowds today who never clearly think out an issue; heedlessly thoughtless people who are led by practical, hard-headed men to whom idealism is silly twaddle; or by narrowly religious people who resent innovations, are impatient of new ideas, or in their hearts are as suspicious of ideals as any of the cynical people who profess no religion.

It is for this reason that the sin of Calvary has a special meaning for men of today.

Who crucified Christ? The people who sent Him to the cross were exactly like the people of today, acting from similar motives, animated by like prejudices. Who were they? The Pharisees—the "good" people of their day who were meticulous in the performance of religious duties, but narrow and bigoted, with prejudices they regarded as sacred convictions; suspicious of Jesus and fearful of His attitude toward accepted tenets of religion. The Apostles were earnest men, eager in following a new religious experience; the Pharisees were men hardened into a set mould and blindly refusing to examine the teaching of the new Master.

Who crucified Him? The Sadducees, who were business ecclesiastics, who felt that in interfering with their temple concessions Jesus was guilty of a high-handed attitude toward a trade which they regarded as legitimate. To interfere with this must not be permitted.

Who crucified Him? Pilate the politician, an easy master who worshipped power; a timid ruler mixed up in corrupt politics and not daring to show that his soul was his own; a weak man who tried to remain neutral and sought to compromise, and felt that he showed power by a sneer at the Jews and a petty gesture of defiance.

Who crucified Him? The people who acclaimed Him on Palm Sunday and became victims of mob psychology five days later.

For whom did Jesus pray? Not for the soldiers only, who were crucifying Him; nor for Pilate only, who knew that for envy He had been betrayed; nor only for the priests and rulers who had hounded Him to death; but for that disappointed, cheated holiday crowd, and for all the world of careless, thoughtless, heedless people, in all ages, who are indifferent to truth, and unappreciative of high ideals, and ignorant of the meaning of faithful, unselfish service, and ready to take their religious ideas second-hand.

For whom did He pray? For the people at Calvary, yes—and for each of us when we align ourselves with those who sneer at ideals and are crassly practical; for us when we side with those who distort moral truth and becloud moral issues; for us who are "herd-minded" and follow leaders without thinking; for us, when in church matters as well as in civic opinions we fail to use what minds we have and are blinded by prejudice.

For whom did He pray? Alas! for the Church people of His day. For not only did wealth, dignity, power, and learning reject Christ, but the religion of His day denied Him. The sin of Calvary comes with a searching test to us who are the Church people of this day. Now and then I have the opportunity to sit with the congregation in church. I always leave wondering, not that so few people attend public worship, but that so many continue the practice. I look about the congregation and wonder what they really believe and how hard they believe it. I ask what most of them really think of Christ's way of life.

And I ask it of myself. I wonder what would happen if I were less oppressed by the business of diocesan administration, and had the courage to make a great act of faith and proclaim Christ as I really know Him. I wonder, when now and then I do speak plainly about religion in this modern American day, whether the tone and temper of Church people is not such that they placard my "prophesying" as pessimistic complaining and write me down a common scold. I wonder whether there may not be this of truth in the condemnation—that many of us who criticize have not the flaming courage to act, rather than merely to talk. I wonder whether we of the Church are not most in need of conversion—both clergy and people—and I ask how much our indifference and "the sloth and ease of Zion" hurts the cause of the kingdom and calls for the Father's forgiveness. You ask how your sin hurts God?

When Jesus came to Golgotha, they hanged Him on a
tree,
And drove great nails through hands and feet, and
made a Calvary;
They crowned Him with a crown of thorns; red were
His wounds and deep;
For those were crude and cruel days, and human flesh
was cheap.

When Jesus came to London town, they simply passed
Him by;
They did not touch a hair of Him, they simply let
Him die;
For men had grown more tender and they would not
give Him pain;
They only just passed down the street and left Him
in the rain.

Still Jesus cried, Forgive them, for they know not what
they do;
And still it rained the winter rain that drenched Him
through and through.
The crowd went home and left the street without a
soul to see,
And Jesus crouched against a wall and cried for
Calvary.*

What is it, then, that we want if we (now and then) realize the sin of our indifference,

---

* Studdert-Kennedy.

our carelessness, our low ideals, our selfishness? This is not an ordinary congregation such as I have described; you are present in church because for today, at least, you are ready to face the fact that sin is here and that sin is tragic.

The only idea of Christianity which some people have today is that in Jesus we have a beautiful example of human goodness. Of course. But that isn't enough, is it? The difficulty is, that the more we think of this example, the harder the Christian life becomes. You hear people say that the Sermon on the Mount is the heart of the Gospel. It is not. Gospel means good news; and the Sermon on the Mount, of itself, would be bad news, if nothing followed. It sets up so high a standard that we could not have the heart to try, if there did not go with it what is the real heart of the Gospel—the promise of divine forgiveness, the offer of divine help, the grace of God-given sacraments, the assurance of the many mansions of the spiritual realm.

The truth is, the Christian life is hard and we haven't tried to live it. Think of it, and you will know your sin and your need of forgiveness.

And when you know your sin, what do you want then? Some good-natured person to tell you that after all it doesn't make much difference; or, at least, that somehow it is going to be "made all right"? Isn't it true that you need someone to tell you that it *does* matter? Don't you want some one to show you that in spite of the hurt you have given he will keep on loving you, and believing in you, and trusting you, and standing by you?

The terrible thing about sin—and you see it in this happy-go-lucky generation of ours that will not think about such a fact as sin really being sin—the terrible thing is, that it kills our faith, faith in ourselves, and faith in human nature, as well as faith in God. A generation ago, faith in God had been given up by many, but there was still faith in humanity. Now that is going. What we need, then, is something to restore faith in ourselves. And we have it in this word from the cross which shows us that God cares, and yet forgives, because God is like Jesus Christ.

You could never learn of God's love from a book. You cannot learn it from an institution. Philosophy cannot reason you into accepting it as a fact. Theological argument will not prove it. The only thing that can make it real is to find living assurance of it in terms of human life. We see the forgiveness of God, the love of God, the enduring trust of God, in the Christ who is incarnate and touches us through a pierced hand and a bruised body and a broken heart with its cry, "Father, forgive them, for they know not what they do."

THE SECOND WORD

Paradise for a Penitent

"To-day shalt thou be with Me in paradise." St. Luke xxiii: 43.

PARADISE FOR A PENITENT

I IMAGINE the man was a social revolutionist; a political agitator, perhaps. Think of him as the sort of man we used to see in Madison Square, standing on a box and exhorting the crowd; a man who would work himself into a frenzy at socialistic meetings. He was, we may suppose, a Galilean revolutionary, hating Rome and Roman domination; intensely national, burning with indignation at the people's wrongs, a mistaken enthusiast whose enthusiasm had degenerated into hatred of law and order.

He had become a member of some roving band of robbers—possibly one of the bands that infested the Jericho road—men full of a sense of rankling injustice, rebels against the social order who had persuaded themselves that it was just and right, as self appointed champions of the poor, to rob the rich—to take what one could of all who could well afford to be relieved of their superfluous possessions.

He would gladly have joined the army of such a Messiah as the people wanted and expected. Meanwhile he had been won into hero worship of some strong robber-leader, perhaps a lesser arch-political agitator like Barabbas, a man to whom he gave a boyish admiration and eager support. They lived on the road by swift raids on traveling caravans and occasional attacks on rich villagers. Then one day they were foolishly incautious. Now two of the men were suffering the due reward of their deeds.

It was a fine piece of cynicism on Pilate's part to crucify two such men with Jesus who was called the Christ. Two purposes were served. The priests were aggravated and annoyed, as Pilate well knew. And it was a splendid opportunity to give warning to others who thought of agitating against the government or living by raids upon legitimate trade and commerce.

So the Man who was the true Messiah, bent on establishing a spiritual kingdom, and the men who would readily have followed a revolutionary Messiah in the effort to restore a world kingdom—they were hanging together. The Pharisees mocked at the "Messiah" they had brought to grief. The priests wagged their heads in derision. The crowd jeered.

At first both the robbers joined in the cries of the crowd, cursing over their own pain but cursing as loudly at the Victim who hung between them. They had no use for a namby-pamby King like this; the times called for sterner measures than such a leader would approve.

Then one of the men, as he watched the Sufferer by his side, began to think. His thinking led him far. He began to feel that his whole career of crime had been a tragically foolish mistake. Some contempt for the fickle crowd penetrated his brain as the numbing effect of the drugged draught of wine they had given him wore off. Some words which as a boy he had heard in the synagogue came back to him. A prayer he had said at his mother's knee was recalled. Contempt of the crowd changed to pity as he heard Jesus pray that they might be forgiven.

Then he thought back over his life since he had been captivated by the boldness of the leader of his robber band—perhaps following him in a spirit of boyish adventure, perhaps attached to him by some story of social injustice that had made his hero an outcast. Now he looked at this other Leader and began to wonder whether he had not, at last, met a hero whom he could really respect, one who was large-hearted and magnanimous, as well as brave. He began to feel that his old hero-worship was misplaced.

Then misunderstanding of Jesus changed into a growing appreciation of the truths for which Jesus suffered. The Kingdom—yes, it must mean spiritual power. And if it was to be the reign of truth, the entrance into the realm of the spirit, then one must become a citizen of the Kingdom through penitence.

Soon he made his acknowledgment of sin and sorrow. He rebuked his companion in crime. Why mock at the Man Jesus? At any rate He had done no wrong, even if He were a mistaken idealist. They were suffering the due reward of their deeds; but the other victim was an innocent victim.

Then came the sudden act of faith, "Lord, remember me, when Thou comest into Thy Kingdom." And our Lord's quick response, "Today shalt thou be with Me in paradise." That shows the way Jesus dealt with foolish, misguided, deluded, sinful men.

Are we sympathetically helpful with mistaken people? The penitent robber was an outcast who had forfeited all consideration; yet here was a Man who (instinctively he knew it) would treat him with kindly consideration. He had been hardly treated, and had grown hard himself, an Ishmaelite, his hand against every man and every man's hand against him. Now he was treated differently—or knew he would be, if Jesus could forgive the sin of priests and people —and he was softened. Jesus would surely know that he wanted to change, even at this belated day. And Jesus *did* know, and accepted the penitent appeal.

That was always His way with people. Zacchaeus, the publican, was a rich rogue; yet he was not altogether bad, or he would not have been so anxious to see the Man who claimed to be the Messiah. Jesus was passing by on the Jericho road, and Zacchaeus, who was little of stature, climbed up into a tree to look over the heads of the crowd. He was a ridiculous figure. The boys who (like himself) had climbed trees to catch sight of the alleged Messiah tittered at him; the girls giggled; their elders (provided their taxes were paid and they had nothing to fear) sneered. Then Jesus looked up, and saw him, and said, "Zacchaeus, hurry now and come down; I must be your guest at dinner today." Is it any wonder that Zacchaeus stood out before the crowd and pledged his fortune and his future in renewal of life? "This Man trusts me," he seems to say; "He believes in me; He has openly accepted me as a friend. Today I make a new start; I mean to become worthy of His friendship."

Do you remember the story of the Passer-by in *The Third Floor Back*—how he came to that London boarding house of middle-class respectability; found a group of lodgers who were petty, mean, selfish, dishonest, scheming; and how he refused to believe that these were their real traits; how he insisted on finding the good in them until at last they found it themselves; and then left them, changed into the likeness of what He believed them to be? Jesus Christ is the great Passer-by. He was ever drawing out the best in men.

It has been beautifully said that there is hardly a roadside pond or pool that is only the dull, brown, muddy thing we suppose it to be. It has as much of the blue sky in it as above it. If we look down deep enough, we see the waving of the green grass which borders the pool, the bending of the leafy boughs above, the passing reflection of the fleecy clouds. So human hearts have something of good in them, however black they seem, and Jesus seeks to draw it out. So misguided men are often *only* misguided, not wilfully wrong-headed; they mean to go the right way, if only some one will be patient with them till they make the turn.

Are we, in these days of class misunderstanding, endeavoring by our sympathetic helpfulness to clear the air? Do we contribute to better feeling and aid in winning over the mistaken and the foolish? How much of patience have we with the blundering efforts of those who *know* that something is wrong somewhere and yet can do no more than kick against the pricks?

And how does suffering affect us? We know that some of the social outcasts of to-day became what they are because life was hard. Then life grows a little difficult for *us* —how do *we* bear up under it?

The penitent thief was purified by suffering. When life was ebbing away, he made his sudden leap to faith. Suffering is a sacrament. It requires right disposition in those who endure it, just as the sacraments of the Church are grace and glory to those who come with right disposition; and are condemnation to those who approach irreverently, thoughtlessly, with gay nonchalance.

One thief was hardened by his cross; the other softened. One reviled Jesus to the end; the other turned to Him in prayer. Teach me, O Lord, rightly to accept all Thou dost send me. Hallow every bereavement, every hardship, every trial, every temptation, that out of my weakness I may learn to seek Thy strength. In every time of suffering or sorrow, touch my heart and sanctify it. Heal my mistakes; overcome my foolish blunders; correct my faults and sins, even though it be on a cross of pain. Only—purify me, and grant that at the end I may die with Thee, and then live with Thee in the paradise of God.

We have prayed for ourselves that we may know how to meet life's hard blows. Do you realize that the way in which we face the difficult things of life may prove our best way of winning others? Christians are the only Bible the world reads today, and if we would win others to faith it must be, in large measure, because of what they see in our lives. How did Jesus win that deluded young agitator? Simply because there was something in Him so splendidly heroic that the man capitulated to His spell. In that hour of weakness and collapse there was not a single sign of anything that was not strong and true, and it made the thief believe just to see how Jesus met death.

There is a sublime simplicity about it. Here, for the moment, Christianity is narrowed down to two persons—our Lord on the cross and the man at His side. Everything in the past is buried. The words of Christ have died away. His miracles are forgotten. His disciples have fled. There is nothing to which He may look forward. He is slowly breathing His life away.

And yet He won.

I do not know of anything finer than the way in which Jesus won a man like this young robber. And remember he was not the only man who was won that day. A Roman soldier stood looking on, and he was won also—this man whose very trade dealt with death. What can be finer than to know that the men who saw Jesus Christ die came to believe in Him because of the way in which He died?

There are plain people all about us—men like the centurion and the penitent thief—who can be brought to belief if they discover that our religion is not a mere matter of custom or convention, a respectable inheritance, but that it is the strength by which we live. Men and women are constantly meeting reverses in life. And what follows? They desert the Church, neglect the sacraments, stop praying, grow cynical and hard. Why? Because they lack even a small portion of the courage of Christ. He did not come to make life easy; He came to make men great. They will not be great. They will not serve God for naught.

And then you see other men and women to whom life is a post which nothing can make them desert. They meet misunderstanding, face sorrow, endure suffering, are compelled to surrender all that seems to make life worth living; and we see them suffering not a word of complaint or self-pity to escape them, putting all the old-time faithfulness into their obligations, calm and careful as in the days before their hearts seemed dead. As we watch them our hearts are filled with the wonder of the cross of Christ.

Oh, what a splendid thing it would be

for us, if it should happen that some doubting and perplexed soul could reach sure faith through the faith they find in our hearts! What a glory if one person could be won through our steadfastness! What a triumph beyond words, if at the last great day we shall discover that some one saw the light of truth in our faces, as in our darkness we walked toward Christ, the Light of the World!

THE THIRD WORD

Providing for His Mother

"When Jesus therefore saw His mother, and the disciple standing by whom He loved, He saith unto His mother, Woman, behold thy son! Then saith He to the disciple, Behold thy mother! And from that hour that disciple took her unto his own home." St. John XIX: 26-27.

PROVIDING FOR HIS MOTHER

E HAVE reason to be specially thankful for this word, it is so thoughtful, so tender, so gracious.

The man who has great things to do is apt to be forgetful in the lesser duties of life. The public man, concerned with large affairs of State; the reformer, pursuing a splendid ideal; the business man, who may truly have a vision of what he wishes to make of his business as a great humanitarian organization, not merely a large financial or industrial corporation; the philanthropist, mapping out a program of social amelioration—how apt they are to have little time for wife or children; how often they are forgetful of social amenities; how frequently they offend in small ways that alienate their friends and antagonize their fellow-workers; how generally do they show lack of considerateness, in countless ways and on innumerable occasions! They may work in a splendid isolation, but it ends in social aloofness.

Our Lord was, necessarily, a public man, living a public life. He was what we would call in our day a social and religious reformer.

Did that mean that His mother felt sometimes that she had lost Him? Did she feel that He seemed always to be moving out of her life? Others in the household failed to understand Him, and even His brethren said that He was "beside Himself." We cannot believe that she ever shared their feeling. She always showed an instinctive, if imperfect, appreciation of His purpose. "Whatsoever He saith unto you, do it." She "kept all these things, and pondered them in her heart." But, probably no mother ever quite understands her son, and though Mary was not like other women, there were times when she must have trusted to instinct, and did not understand.

It is the common lot of mothers to feel that their children are drifting out of their lives. They feel it even more keenly as the children enter into larger activities. Their lot is bound to be, in some measure, lonely, as their sons grow into manhood and take up life's tasks. That is why they cherish mementoes of babyhood days and early childhood —toys the boy used, school books which bear the marks of hard wear, if not of hard study, photographs of the boy when he was little. Somewhere, the other day, I saw the question asked, "Did Mary treasure the little hammer with which the Child Jesus learned His trade?"

So we should like to know about the Virgin Mother. Was her sense of loss as keen as the ordinary mother's? Was it, perhaps, keener? Just because of the greatness of His work, did she miss Jesus the more? When messengers went to Him to say that His mother and His brethren were seeking Him, did she feel a little hurt as the report came that He had looked about on those whom He was teaching and had said, "Behold My mother and My brethren"? Somebody, surely, told her about that, and like most people who are ready to impart unwelcome news, very likely they neglected to add that He had also said, "Whosoever shall do the will of God, the same is My brother, and My sister, and My mother." Even if they told this as well as the rest, perhaps it sounded to Mary a little coldly impersonal! Perhaps she remembered how Simeon had predicted that a sword would pierce her own soul. The prediction may not have had reference only to the tragic loss on the Day of Crucifixion. There were other times of sword-piercing.

And she had borne so much for Him! Think of what she took upon her heart when she accepted her sacred calling and answered the angelic salutation with her word of consent, "Be it unto me according to thy word." We know there must have been a breath of scandal, until Joseph, one of God's gentlemen, took her away from the gossip of the village.

And, again, we feel sure that she did not know all the mystery of her Son's birth. We know that the fulness of understanding of His divine personality must have come slowly to her, as it came slowly to others.

We know that even the work of His ministry must have been in some degree beyond her comprehension. Her life must have been lonely as His ministry engaged His activities more and more.

We want to know, then, something clear and definite of our Lord's relationship with His mother, and we are glad to have this word.

Not that it is in any way surprising to learn that He thought of her at the end. After all, when we stop to think, we know we should expect something just like this. We know that He was always beautifully human, and so we know that He could never have failed her, however great His work and however absorbing.

We could guess it because He was always so lovable, likable, considerate, and friendly with others. We remember the picture of Him as He walked the friendly road with His disciples, talking with them of the things of earth until they glowed with the glory of heaven, living with them in the intimacy of daily life, sleeping with them under the evening stars; ever compassionate to those whose sin-sick souls and diseased bodies He restored into harmony with the beautiful nature that lay round about them.

We expect, therefore, this word to His mother and to the disciple whom He loved. Only—we are glad to have it.

And we are glad that it was uttered just when it was. For hours He had been hanging upon the cross. Now there was approaching the terrible time of darkness. Some of the people were leaving. There was a lull in the excitement. The women of Galilee were standing afar off, and they would soon be leaving, too. Only His mother and John the Beloved were near the cross, and He did not want her to see His extremity of suffering. He must hasten the parting.

And so, though there was a world of interests to which He must give thought, though He was in an extremity of pain, though the desolation of the cross was soon to fall upon Him till He seemed forsaken of the Father, though He was wrestling with the problems of life and death, and sin and evil—He sinks self in the thought of His mother's future and provides for her care by His dearest friend; and He shows, as well, His deepest trust in that friend by giving him the sweetest task that trust and affection could ever find for him.

It must mean that this was typical of the whole life relationship of Jesus and the Blessed Mother. The scene on Calvary reflects what must have been characteristic of the home life of Nazareth.

Now. What about our home life? A famous American humorist has asked, "What is the use of having a family, if you can't be disagreeable in the bosom of it?" There are fathers who must have unconsciously accepted that as the motto of the domestic circle! Not so many mothers, of course! And there are children who do not understand what a debt they owe to parental love and self sacrifice. Some of you younger people who are here—I beg you to think of that!

Indeed, think of our home life, in general, in America. It does no good, it "gets us nowhere," merely to complain that steam radiators have replaced hearthstones, or that homes have often become little more than places where we sleep some small part of the night. As plain matter of fact, we can make a home in a top story of a huge apartment house, if we try. This is not, therefore, a complaint. It is a plea to parents and their children alike. It is a plea to parents to try earnestly to make home a real home; to seek seriously to understand the expanding life of their sons and daughters; to enter into their life; to keep pace with their interests. And it is a plea to the young people. You who are here may translate the words of the preacher into your own special vocabulary and pass it on to others who are not here. Ask them whether, if they have fairly decent parents, they need always be heady and head-strong. Ask them, if they feel that their parents are not quite what they should be, whether wisdom may not be learned out of the heart of youth as well as from "the mouths of babes and sucklings." Ask them whether, in their craze for reality and directness, for utter sincerity and blunt straightforwardness, in their pardonable impatience with smugness and cant, they are quite sure they are not losing some things fine and beautiful. Isn't the great lack of to-day the almost total loss of courtesy and thoughtfulness and kindly consideration? Is there any virtue in being "hard-boiled"? Why encase ourselves in a covering of pretended indifference and sophistication? Why not cultivate the finer qualities? Why be ashamed of a family affection that will "let itself go"?

At any rate, *some* of you have people at home who care. And some day, with aching hearts, you may look back on other days—days of missed opportunities which you would give everything in the world not to have misused or neglected.

That much for sons and daughters. And you mothers—here is a sentence I have copied down for you from some forgotten source. It reads: "Isn't it strange that in modern social life there are so many women who will join half a dozen societies for ameliorating the lot of the unfortunate, and have never yet learned to specialize in the loving care of those who are peculiarly their own?"

I ask another question of the men—two questions, in fact: "Isn't it strange that husbands will study the tastes of those with whom they do business, and forget that the woman at home would possibly be happier if *her* tastes were studied? Isn't it strange how keenly you will try to read the mind of a business rival or associate, without dreaming of the close-at-hand duty of endeavoring to read the mind of your own boy?"

Almighty and most loving God, our heavenly Father, give us grace ever to be tender and thoughtful toward those whom Thou hast bound together in the ties of family life. Give us understanding, wider sympathy, and larger patience, that we may ever be considerate and unselfish. Make our homes happy with the joy that Thou alone canst give; homes more like that of the Holy Family where Jesus was a loving Son and Brother, Mary an understanding mother, and Joseph the ever-chivalrous husband, simple, noble, loyal, who knew how to love a woman and protect her. So shall our homes be places of preparation for that Home which is to be, eternal in the heavens, where we shall know Him who is divine, and yet (even there) divinely human: Thy Son, Jesus Christ our Lord. Amen.

THE FOURTH WORD

The Cry of Desolation

"Now from the sixth hour there was darkness over all the land unto the ninth hour. And about the ninth hour Jesus cried with a loud voice, Eli, Eli, lama sabachthani? That is to say, My God, My God, why hast Thou forsaken Me?" St. Matthew XXVII: 45-46.

THE CRY OF DESOLATION

DARKNESS was sweeping down upon the three crosses, the presage of the earthquake of which record is given. The air was sultry. The sky was dull, yellow, copper-colored. Occasionally the face of the Sufferer showed distinctly in the gloom. Those who looked seem to have been strangely moved; for we read that they began to return to the city, "smiting upon their breasts," the earlier excitement ending in terror.

During these hours the Saviour hung in agony. Out of the darkness, well toward the end of His suffering, there rang out a cry of anguish: "My God, My God, why hast Thou forsaken Me?"

There is one thing which we of the clergy, and you who are Christian believers, ought, in these days, to recognize more clearly and honestly. It is this: that faith is no easy matter.

For many men, the vastness of the universe, man's seeming relative insignificance, the difficulties of the Bible, the doubts about miracles, a host of like problems—above all, the presence of sin, sorrow, suffering, and death in a world supposed to be ruled by a Loving Father—all these things make it hard to believe. You remember the words of George Tyrrell, who struggled for faith, always loyal to his vision, though not orthodox in his profession, suffering excommunication, coughing out his lungs on the edge of starvation, crying out his essential belief and praying to be helped in his unbelief: "To believe that this terrible machine world is really from God, in God, and unto God, that through it and in spite of its blind fatality all things work together for good—that is faith in long trousers; the other is faith in knickerbockers." Not mere childish faith, but an adult faith that has faced facts, and has struggled on, and agonized, and gripped hard, and held fast; faltered, fallen, risen, struggled on again, refused to let go altogether, at last seen light.

I do not see how any clergyman who has tried to minister to people in their trouble, or trial, or sorrow, and has heard them say again and again, "Why does God permit it?" —I do not see how any such pastor can fail to have sympathy with doubt. Nor can I understand his failing to see how it may strengthen the doubter, if he can be made to understand that this word from the cross shows that Jesus had an experience akin to his own, and yet triumphed.

We must get it out of our minds that there is necessarily something wrong with us when we have doubts. Unquestionably, loss of faith sometimes issues out of the loss of moral earnestness and failure of any real effort in prayer and devotion. But sometimes our doubts are reachings toward light; sometimes the pains of our deepest questionings are growth pains. "The only doubt that damns," somebody has said, "is the doubt that does not fight on, the doubt that prides itself in denial, glories in its own supposed intellectual superiority, and is cynically careless in disturbing the faith of others."

I call you to consider this cry of desolation, because it shows us that there is that in Jesus Christ which expresses understanding of our trouble, and I remind you, moreover, that if we have the right faith in Christ it means that we believe also in a God who has entered into the tragedy of human life and sympathizes.

The wonderful thing about the Gospels—I have already said this, but I repeat it—is their transparent honesty. Here in the record of this word is an honesty that carries conviction of the essential truthfulness of the story of Christ. No one could have invented the word. No one but a sincerely accurate witness would have dared to record it. Picture it! You are telling about the death of a good man who has been your friend and leader, to whom you have given all your loyalty and love, and the only word you record as spoken in his last hours is a word like this! Yet, though we have in the record seven words from the cross, this is the only one to be found in the primitive Gospel —that of St. Mark; it is the only one incorporated in the longer account of the passion in the First Gospel.

Today a good many people are troubled over the new way in which critics treat the Gospels. It seems to them that they have been robbed of almost all that is precious. But criticism has in many ways made the Gospels more natural and more real. And criticism has done nothing to mar the beauty of the Central Figure. Criticism, in fact, often makes the story more credable; certainly it cannot touch its real essence. Nothing can make us lose our certainty that here we have the testimony of honest eye-witnesses, whatever may be our theory of how the record was made or through whose hands we have received it. Here, in this word, you certainly reach reality.

And here, also, in the most primitive account of the passion, you see that these early records bear witness to the belief that the death of Jesus was no ordinary death. It shows a Saviour bearing the burden of the world's sin.

This word is a quotation. It comes from the Twenty-second Psalm.

I wonder whether that does not prove that in the dark hours of His agony Jesus was engaged in prayer and meditation. Of what was He thinking? What voices spoke to Him above the jeering cries of the crowd? Did He remember how His ministry had begun with the greeting of John the Baptist, "Behold the Lamb of God, which taketh away the sin of the world"? He Himself had told men that He came as a suffering Messiah; was He meditating on those difficult words of the ancient prophet: "He is despised and rejected of men; a man of sorrows, and acquainted with grief. Surely he hath borne our griefs and carried our sorrows. He was wounded for our transgressions, he was bruised for our iniquities; the chastisement of our peace was upon him; and with his stripes we are healed. The Lord hath laid on him the iniquity of us all"—was He searching the meaning of words like those?

At any rate, we may be sure that He was repeating, for His strength and consolation, some of the psalms out of the "hymn book" of His people; for He must have been saying this Twenty-second Psalm, and the opening words of the psalm rang out in a loud voice, as a sharper pang marked His agony.

That gives a hint to us in our distress. When doubts assail, go back to the Source of Strength. When prayer is difficult, keep on praying. You can, at least, say with the doubter of old, "O God, if there be a God, save my soul, if I have a soul."

But you can venture on a better prayer than that. Because the God we worship is the God revealed on Calvary. The Christian faith declares that in spite of all things that shriek denial, God is like Jesus Christ. He is not a sort of Magnified Man, sitting in the center of the universe, ruling things and judging people; He is a God who enters into the tragedy of life; He knows and cares.

> 'Tis the weakness in strength, that I cry for! my flesh that I seek
> In the Godhead! I seek and I find it. Oh, Saul, it shall be
> A face like my face that receives thee; a Man like to me

Thou shall love and be loved by, for ever: a Hand like
this hand
Shall throw open the gate of new life to thee! See the
Christ stand! *

The way out of doubt is to follow Christ. "They were in the way going up to Jerusalem, and Jesus went before them, and they were amazed, and as they followed they were afraid." But they did follow—that is the main thing. If you have doubts, look through all the wisdom of the world, and you will find no one like Him to follow. If all the puzzled people in the world would stop for a while their present never-ceasing effort to explain all difficulties, and just follow, doubts would disappear.

That is the way Peter, with all his weakness, after all his denial, came back at the last. It was because he had the *following* spirit. When Jesus asked him, "Will ye also go away?" he spoke out of his doubt and difficulty: "To whom shall we go? Thou hast the words of eternal life, and we believe and are sure that Thou art the Christ, the Son of the living God."

* Browning's *Saul.*

And do not forget that with Jesus there was no lack of faith. If this word is the sharp cry of prayer as He repeated the psalm in devotion, then while it shows the agony of His desolation and the fulness of His entrance into human tragedy, nevertheless it shows Him standing firm and without wavering. Assuredly we are right in saying that Jesus never doubted; He was tempted to doubt, but triumphed.

That readiness to stand, and not to waver, will be a part of our following of Christ. Don't forget it. If ever there was a time when Christianity needed the revival of this spirit of heroic allegiance, it is now.

Sometimes it may seem that we are called upon to stand without divine help, but it is really at hand, if we seek it. The sense of desolation may be the result of past sin and indifference; but it may also be God's way of testing the bravery of our endurance. It may be, as it was with our Lord, the road to peace and supreme blessing.

At any rate, we know this: that sometimes, whether we have peace and comfort or not, even though we have little sense of God's presence and help, and prayers are dry and devotion dead, we must keep on. Those who persistently stand for truth simply must rely on God; for often they must stand alone, with none but Him to call upon.

Are you willing to do it?

In religion, for example. The world has little ability to apprehend spiritual things; and yet how often we allow our own faith to evaporate because of the lack of clear faith around us. We thought we knew, and then we become upset and disturbed, because somebody else talked of his doubts; someone, in all likelihood, who had given no real thought to the matter, yet somehow expected religious truth to trickle into his mind without effort on his part.

In the Church. There is a false liberality abroad in these days, and the things once most surely believed are counted of little worth. If we protest, we risk the charge of narrowness and pettiness; we are supposed to be enemies of tolerance and liberality. Can we stand alone?

Of course we must be on our guard

against mere obstinacy. But if we feel sure we are right, we *must* stand steadfast. Time will make truth clear—and often the time of revelation is not far distant. History has vindicated many a brave man whom his own generation condemned. Are many of you ready to wait for the verdict of history?

In society. There are social customs now which demand of Christian believers courage of conviction and strength of endurance. Jesus Christ followed truth and right, though He was led to Calvary and the cross. Have you even a little of His bravery?

> Once to every man and nation
> Comes the moment to decide,
> In the strife of truth with falsehood,
> For the good or evil side.
>
> * * * * * *
>
> Then it is the brave man chooses
> While the coward stands aside,
> Till the multitude make virtue
> Of the faith they had denied.*

---

* James Russell Lowell.

THE FIFTH WORD

Patient Endurance of Pain

"After this, Jesus knowing that all things were now accomplished, that the Scripture might be fulfilled, saith, I thirst. Now there was set a vessel full of vinegar; and they filled a sponge with vinegar, and put it upon hyssop, and put it to His mouth." St. John XIX: 28-29.

PATIENT ENDURANCE OF PAIN

A STRIKING feature of the Gospel narratives is their repression and restraint. The Evangelists tell the story simply and quickly, without comment or ejaculation. The facts speak for themselves. This is partly because there is so much to record that the narrative must be brief. We know, now, that the Gospels are made up of the Sayings of Jesus, His Parables, brief records of His Wonderful Works, short reports of Dialogues which more fully explain His teaching, and notes of His Passion, with similar short records of His Resurrection appearances. They were probably written in this brief form, because they were first given orally for ready memorizing. Their very brevity made them more easily remembered.

Yet we cannot but feel that the restraint of the record is due, in part, to the fact that the disciples lived in such an atmosphere of reverence as would forbid ejaculatory comment. The wonder of His life, as a whole, compelled brevity of treatment of special events. And this brevity gives dignity and majestic impressiveness to the main story.

In the account of the passion this restraint is specially noticeable. Much might have been told of the sufferings of the Divine Victim, but it is all too big for that. There is only the bare record of the facts. There is no attempt to dwell upon the special cruelty of the executioners in nailing Him to the cross. There is only the bare mention of the soldiers' mockery of the Prisoner whose Crucifixion Placard declared that He was executed for His kingly claims. Herod's jesting act in arraying Him in royal robes is dismissed with a sentence.

Calvary's story makes no attempt to harrow our feelings. There was the Agony of the Garden, the three hurried hearings before Caiaphas and Annas; the three public trials in the court of Pilate and Herod; the scourging with the Roman whips of leather tipped with lead; the thorny crown; the indignity of the spitting; the bearing of the heavy shoulder-beam of the cross; the fall by the wayside; the crucifixion itself; the hours of torture; the suffering in the darkness. And only one word hints at the awfulness of this physical agony. Dreadful as that agony was, the agony of thirst swallowed up all the rest. Under the hot sun, with the wounds draining out His life, this was the supreme distress.

Our Lord died as a Hero. A bare recital of the facts shows this—told without comment, or description, or direct appeal to sympathy.

Jesus was no Stoic. His patient endurance of suffering is a constant rebuke to our impatience, our softness, our intolerance of pain; but He was brave, not stoical, and He was not ashamed to speak the word, "I thirst," nor indifferent to the pity of the soldiers who soaked the sponge in sour wine, and lifted it to His lips.

The mystery of pain is the greatest mystery of life. Some have rebelled at the harrowing fact of human wretchedness. Some, even if not drawn into rebellion, have been perplexed beyond measure at life's sorrow and suffering. They have asked, "Why did not God, if He is a good God, make the world good and happy, and keep it good and happy?"

And, of course, if we have felt all this when we faced the problem in general, the agony has come home to us with terrible sharpness when we have faced it in our own lives. You all know how great the anguish can be. Parents who are looking upon a sick or dying child, and weeping in their grief, have cried out in brokenhearted distress. The poor, suffering and seeing their dear ones suffer, have uttered their complaint. The sick and crippled and helpless, in keener anguish than flesh can bear, have cried out their eternal "Why?" to God. All of you who are here today have at some time or other faced the same agonizing question yourselves, if not in your own lives, at least in the lives of those who are close to you. You came here to this church today, some of you, through streets that were dark with tragedy, and realizing (if you stopped to think) something of the hopeless illness that could be found in the homes of the rich and in the homes of the poor; tragedies attested by what you could read in the haggard faces of some of the people you passed on the way. At some time or other you have been overwhelmed by the sadness of life, a pathos so great that only infinite pity can cope with it.

What suggestions do we discover from the faith which is in Christ Jesus as to this problem of pain? The first thing to which I want to call your attention is this remarkable fact, that the men in whom the Christian faith first had its expression, the men with whom the Christian faith began and through whom it spread, proclaimed that faith—it was faith in a Loving Father—*in the face of the world's worst tragedy.*

I wonder whether we always remember that. We have had to hold our faith fast, and sometimes we succeed in holding it fast because (practically speaking) we have never dared to face all of the facts. Do we realize that this faith in which we proclaim our belief had its very origin in history's most appalling tragedy? It sprang out of the Cross of Calvary. It was proclaimed by men who had faced facts as nobody else in the world had ever faced facts before. It was accepted by men who believed despite the tragedy of life of which they had suffered such bitter experience. They were men who believed because—now note this—because they had seen love at last triumph over sin and suffering and evil. They believed because they felt that they had seen God in Jesus Christ. And so they *knew*—they knew that God was love, even though they could not understand.

So remember, first of all, the striking fact that this faith of ours, in which we proclaim our trust in a Loving God, despite everything in the world which seems to cry against it—remember that this faith sprang out of the world's worst tragedy.

Then, secondly, it is significant that men have held their faith in a Loving God, because they have learned from their Lord and Master Jesus Christ what is the real purpose of life, namely, *the building of character*. Looking back over the life of their Master, perhaps they saw that if you banish sorrow altogether, you banish sacrificial love; if you banish calamity, you banish courage; if you banish fear, you banish fortitude and triumphant faith; if you abolish the Cross and what the Cross stands for in human life, you abolish the spirit of Jesus Christ in men.

There are many sorrows and trials, of course, that we can never understand; but now and then we do see what sorrows and trials and temptations and difficulties and suffering can make of men. *This is a hard world in which to be perfectly happy, but it is a great world in which to build character.* That was the second great fact that the first followers of Jesus Christ learned from their Master.

And then, one more thing that Jesus Christ shows us, I believe, is that suffering and sorrow may be our greatest means of witnessing for God. It was plainly so in His own case. The penitent robber was won to Christ by the Lord's endurance. Is there anyone who knows us who has ever been brought one whit closer to God by the way in which he has seen us bear life's trials? On the contrary, is it not true that we make our trials an excuse for being selfish and exacting? We are ill, and we seem to regard the fact as sufficient justification for making everybody else uncomfortable. We are obsessed with our own misery. We tell the whole story of our own aches and pains. Someone asks how the doctor found us to-day, and if the doctor were truthful he would reply, "Complaining, as usual."

There is something even more important—something which sums up all I have been trying to say. Jesus Christ never gave any explanation of the problem of pain, though, of course, He was fully aware of it. His trust in a Heavenly Father was no blind faith. He knew that sparrows "fall to the ground," even though He spoke trustfully of the Father's knowledge of their fall. He knew sickness and pain—was He not constantly dealing with them? Yet He proclaimed the Father's love, without explanation of the mystery. It is hopeless to find an explanation. Jesus did something infinitely better; *He showed men how to meet this mystery.*

There are ways in which men refuse to meet the problem. You can fly from it. In one of the Beatitudes, Jesus said, "Blessed are they that mourn." I think He meant, Blessed are they who, instead of shutting their eyes and ears against the sorrow of the world, try to enter into it with sympathetic understanding and love. In that sense it would be quite true if we were to say, "Blessed are they that mourn." There never was a happier day in your life than the day in which you felt sympathetically, until it hurt, the sorrowing and suffering of the world, and tried to enter into it helpfully. There never was a happier day in your life than the day when you were able to bring to somebody else, in his or her trouble, the comfort and peace of the Gospel.

There are people, however, who refuse to enter into the world's suffering and sorrow and will not face it in their own lives. They fly from it. They avoid every token of its approach. They shut it out whenever, and as long, as they possibly can. I suppose to a certain extent we are justified in doing that. We dare not allow the imagination to picture too vividly the sorrow of the world. If we were to do so, it would be as if nature were to unstop our ears so that we could hear the grass grow and the squirrel's heart beat. Someone has said that if that happened we should go mad in the roar that lies just the other side of silence. So, of course, we would not let the mind dwell too much on the world's suffering and sorrow. To permit too keen a vision of it would be near to madness.

But you will understand what I mean. I mean the tendency to run away in a cowardly unwillingness to face suffering and sorrow. The modern world is altogether too prone to do it. There are drug victims without number, victims of morphia and cocaine and drink, all showing such cowardice. Sometimes they are the very people who are supposed to be professing Christians.

We are not to fly from the world's evil. It is only because of our own experience that we can ever help anybody else. He who has known suffering and sorrow can sympathize with suffering and sorrow. He who knows the hurt in his own heart can bring to others the comfort wherewith he himself has been comforted of God.

I do believe, moreover, that our own sense of the poignancy of the problem of pain suggests a God from whom the thought comes. We may be quite sure, if the love in our own hearts cries out against evil, that there is that in the heart of the Infinite which corresponds to our pain and grief.

Just one more thing, therefore, that the Christian faith tells us with ringing tones: If we believe in Jesus Christ as the Incarnate Son of God, then—whether we ever understand or not, whether through all our days we find ourselves occasionally doubting or not— then we know that God is love, because we have once had the heart of God unveiled in the sight of men. There cannot be any question of the love of Jesus Christ. If He is the perfect unveiling of the Father's heart, then the heart of God is as the heart of Jesus Christ, and we know and believe, though we do not understand. Outside of Jesus Christ I wonder how anybody can be anything but an agnostic, but with Jesus Christ we trust and hope; indeed, I think we can know with moral certainty.

I said at the outset of these addresses that we were to keep to the plain meaning of each of the Words from the Cross, without straining after a mystical interpretation. Will it seem a violation of that promise, if I say that Jesus thirsts now—thirsts for love and service? I do not think so. If He accepted the sympathy of the soldiers, He is as ready to receive our sympathy and service.

And we can give it only in our service of others. "I was thirsty, and ye gave Me drink." "When saw we Thee an hungered and fed Thee? or thirsty and gave Thee drink?" And He replies: "Inasmuch as ye have done it unto one of the least of these My brethren, ye have done it unto Me." Whenever we resolve to make our Christian charity pass beyond stated contributions to community chests and welfare organizations, and endeavor to add our own piece of personal service in bringing to some sick, aged, lonely, or needy soul the touch of sympathy and helpfulness, we lift a comforting draught to our Lord's lips. And yet there are multitudes of Christian people who never visit a hospital ward, or walk through a poor section of the city, or climb a steep staircase, or enter a lonely room, to help one of Christ's hidden brothers and sisters. Try such a piece of personal service as time and other duties permit it. It will bring you new joy and faith and peace. And Jesus has promised that none who so serve Him will lose a reward.

THE SIXTH WORD

The Purpose of Life

"When Jesus therefore had received the vinegar, He said, It is finished." St. John xix: 30.

THE PURPOSE OF LIFE

IT ALL depends upon the tone of voice in which the words were uttered. They may have been spoken as a sigh of resignation; or a sobbing cry of relief; or a glad shout of achievement. I like to think that this last is the true interpretation. Then the words mean that joy was beginning to break through the sorrow. Then they are an exultant, victorious utterance, a declaration of triumph: Work accomplished; His task performed; life's duty fulfilled; His offering perfected.

It all depends upon the tone of voice, I say, and there are indications that this may be the true explanation. St. Luke tells us that the final words with which Jesus commended His soul to the Father were spoken after He had "cried with a loud voice." The last four words came in quick succession, at the very end, and so St. Luke's reference may be to the cry of desolation; but it may be that the final act of trust came after this shout of victory. In that case, we have something more than a mere marking of the end. The word does, of course, mean that the pain was ended, His life over, His work complete, the prophecies fulfilled; but it means that—and more.

So we interpret the word thus: This which looks like a failure is really a glorious success. The work of redemption is done. I have finished all I came to do. I have fulfilled the Father's purpose. Seemingly defeated, I have really succeeded. I came to do Thy will, O God, and I have done it; never swerving a hair's breadth from the path of duty, never hesitating a moment in allegiance and loyal obedience. Since the day when the door of the carpenter's shop closed and I went down to the Jordan, and heard John's call to the nation, and went into the wilderness to map out My life's mission, and came back to the ministry for which I was sent—in all that time nothing has been forgotten, or overlooked, or shirked, or neglected. Looking far back through the years to that earlier day when I said that I must be in My Father's house and about My Father's business, I see a rounded, complete life; a finished work.

Already Jesus seems to see of the travail of His soul, and is satisfied. Already, in the winning of the man at His side, He has proved that, if lifted up, He will draw men unto Himself.

Looked at in this way, the Sixth Word from the Cross shows Jesus Christ's view of life. Life is a vocation, a ministry, a service. So He regarded it when at the age of twelve He showed boyish surprise that the parents did not look for Him at once in the Father's house. So He regarded it when He set His face steadfastly to go to Jerusalem. So He regards it now, when that earthly life is ending.

It has been supposed that the motto of His life expressed the same thought. Every Jewish boy had a birthday text. He learned it as soon as he had learned that other text, "Hear, O Israel, the Lord thy God is one Lord." Enclosed in a shining metal case, and affixed to the door post of the house, this "Mesusah" text was the motto of every devout home. Carried in the parent's arms, the child was taught to touch it, as he saw his father reverently put his own hand on it, kiss the finger, and speak a benediction; "The Lord shall preserve thy going out and thy coming in, from this time forth, and even forevermore." That would have been the first words Jesus learned out of the ancient Writings. Next, I have said, came the learning of a birthday text. May we not suppose that the text given to Jesus was the one whose thought so filled His mind and heart, "I came to do Thy will, O God"?

Life, then, meant to Jesus a ministry and a vocation. It had a purpose and a plan. Do we regard life in that way? If many of us did so regard it, we should be engaged in other work than that which now occupies us. Men would not permit themselves to become so absorbed in business as to forget to be thoughtful husbands and fathers. Women would put into Church work some of the abounding interest they now give to clubs and social duties. Parents might even become so extravagantly religious as to offer no objections if their sons thought of studying for the ministry! Legacies would not be left to every cause under the sun except the Church's work and mission. Above all, we should be learning that the primary objective in life is the building of character. We should be concerned with the things which contribute toward that purpose: prayer, worship, faithful communions, personal service.

There died in this city [New York] at the beginning of this Lenten season a great leader in American business life, a man* who had made the corporation of which he was the head the largest financial organization in the world. But he had made it much more than that: a great humanitarian organization. He was very dear to me —a second father, regarding me as his son— and I may be permitted, perhaps, to pay this brief tribute to his memory. He was a great and good man, as great in faith as any man I have ever known. He regarded his busi-

* Mr. Haley Fiske.

ness as the field in which he was to express his Christian faith. He died quietly, just after he had come home from Holy Communion and later worship in church. It was a fitting death for one who always thought of his business career as a vocation, and always sought divine grace that he might translate into his everyday life the faith by which he tried to live. I know that he prayed for guidance in business decisions, that in his prayers he remembered his business associates, that every new opening in welfare work was undertaken only after divine direction had been sought. How fitting, then, that death should come just as he had left the altar. There, during half a century, he had so often sought light on life's duties!

Would that we might have more men who would regard their day's work in such fashion as a vocation! They would discover, I am sure, that many things done now could not be done if business is to express the spirit of Jesus Christ. Times have changed, and men have long since learned that service in business *pays;* but they have not yet learned what *Christian methods* in business mean.

Certainly they have not learned that business is a divine calling; that it must be so regarded if real Christians are to engage in it. Men may be "called" to a business career just as truly as men are called to the priesthood. Your daily work is your opportunity to manifest your Christianity. As you go about each task, you are, or should be, a Christ-bearer. The religion of an Incarnate Christ is the religion of everyday life. It declares that *all* of life must be permeated and penetrated by the Spirit of God. Unless our Christianity does enter into our daily life, into every part of it, our Christianity is abortive, defective, insincere.

Of course, it is not easy to give to secular life this sense of vocation. Men are hampered by conditions not of their own making. They face competition, and competition is not always fair. In these days they face combinations, and "chain-business," and political entanglements, and a host of other difficulties. It is not easy. Nothing really worth doing is ever easy. Jesus Christ never meant to make life easy. The discovery of duty and the serious effort to perform it will not be easy. But there are other people who have set themselves to the task, and they can tell you that the effort moulds character and makes men.

You see, then, Jesus Christ's view of life. He regarded it as a vocation. He regarded His work as sacred. With us the sense of duty seems to be dulled. We do what we like to do and shirk the rest. Is not the deep and true sense of religious obligation becoming weakened and obscured?

If it were any other day, and we were anywhere else, I suppose you might frankly ask me not to be "always preaching." Has it ever occurred to you that we clergy do not like to preach? I mean, we get tired of a church where the clergy are always expected to do the talking, while the congregation listens. We are fearful lest religion shall evaporate in words. We want a striving, working, loving church. We want men to see the joy of service. We get tired of the necessity of always telling them this. We grow doubtful as to whether they learn much from our continuous talking. For once, then, today, let us all listen—you and I together. As we listen, this is what I hear Jesus Christ say:

The one clear call in life is to prepare in the soul a home for God. The one thing which God put us into the world to do is to build up character. Character is something we cannot keep to ourselves; it is always being communicated. In building a character, therefore, we are helping to build a new world.

Think of the joy and satisfaction of life if we so regard it! It was so that Jesus thought of it; and I feel sure that there must have been in His words, "It is finished," something of the splendor of perfect accomplishment. The weary hours have almost passed; our watch by the cross is nearly over; and just before He passes we hear from a Mighty Worker a triumph-cry of successful service—of work well done.

THE SEVENTH WORD

Departing in Peace

"And when Jesus had cried with a loud voice, He said, Father, into Thy hands I commend My spirit; and having said thus, He gave up the ghost." St. Luke XXIII: 46.

DEPARTING IN PEACE

WE NOTE three things about this last utterance of the Lord Jesus: It is a prayer. The prayer is in words of Holy Scripture. It expresses calm, restful confidence in God His Father.

Jesus passed from life to death with a prayer on His lips, at the very moment of spiritual communion. Though He was dying as a criminal, deserted by his friends, scoffed at by His enemies, suffering intense physical pain, enduring still greater mental anguish, dying after a long and agonizing struggle and at the close of hours of spiritual desolation—yet He fell asleep at the very moment of deepest and fullest devotion, breathing a prayer to His Father, of whose love He was certain and in whose presence He was safe.

The prayer was in words of the Sacred Writings. Through the long hours He had been comforting His heart with such words. We have seen that the cry of desolation was also a prayer of faith, the first words of the Twenty-second Psalm. These words are also from the Jewish "hymnal." They are a part of the Thirty-first Psalm, used afterwards in one of the night offices of the Church, Compline: "Into thy hands I commend my spirit; for Thou hast redeemed me, O Lord, Thou God of truth." It is said that for centuries before the Christian era this psalm had been used in the eventide devotions of pious Hebrews, and that this verse, especially, was repeated by the children in their evening prayers.

There is nothing like the Bible to bring comfort to the troubled and the suffering. Though many things puzzle us, we find in it such thoughts as make us sure that the words are of God. "Let not your heart be troubled; ye believe in God; believe also in Me. In My Father's house are many mansions; if it were not so, I would have told you. I go to prepare a place for you." "Whither I go ye know, and the way ye know." "I am the Way, the Truth, and the

Life." "Blessed are they that mourn; for they shall be comforted." "Come unto Me, all ye that travail, and are heavy laden, and I will give you rest." "Whom the Lord loveth, He chasteneth, and scourgeth every son whom He receiveth." "If we confess our sins, God is faithful and just, to forgive us our sins." "Right dear, in the sight of the Lord, is the death of His saints." "Blessed are the dead who die in the Lord: even so, saith the Spirit; for they rest from their labors." "God so loved the world, that He gave His Only-Begotten Son, that whosoever believeth in Him should not perish, but have everlasting life." No—whatever difficulties we may find in the Bible, we find there devotional treasure.

Finally, the prayer was a prayer of trust, of restful confidence in God as Father. If we cannot make men see, through Christ, that God is a Friendly God, there is something wrong about our Christianity. That is what I have tried to do in today's addresses: to give you this faith and trust, despite our doubts; to make God nearer and to help you to feel His love and care. I have failed in preaching the Cross today, if I have not helped you, at least a little, into this faith and trust of the Lord Jesus. I shall have failed miserably if I cannot make you see how tender and beautiful is this last word, which shows how he believed to the end.

So Jesus died in prayer—a prayer phrased in the words of Holy Scripture—a prayer of trust and peace. That is the way we want to die, is it not, if we *must* think about death?

But the death will be like the life. Our Lord died with a prayer on His lips, because He lived a life of prayer. Think of His long nights of devotion. Think of the times when He rose "a great while before it was day," "while it was yet dark," to commune with the Father. Think of the prayers He used before He asked of Peter the momentous questions, "Who do men say that I am? Who do *you* say that I am?" Think of His prayers for guidance, before He chose the Twelve. Think of His prayer, before He called forth Lazarus from the grave. Think of His prayer in Gethsemane, a prayer which seemed not to be answered, though the answer really came in the gradual disclosure of the Father's will. You see it as the prayer continues: First, "Father, *if it be possible,* let this cup pass from Me." Then: *"If this cup may not pass from Me, except I drink it,* Thy will be done." Think of His great sacerdotal prayer at the Last Supper.

And He was as busy as we are. The crowd pressed Him, so that He had not so much as time to eat. At least once He "sent them away," that He might be alone in prayer.

Somehow, we expect to patch up a friendship with God on the spur of the moment. We are too busy to pray, or too uncertain to keep on; and then we expect that somehow the gift will be given us at the end. It cannot be so. We do not go to some friend of a single day and talk with him naturally about the deep things of life. It is so with our Heavenly Father. We must know Him long in life if we would have Him near in death. If we would die in prayer, we must live in prayer.

And the comfort of the Scriptures. You cannot enter a great library, go to the section where you will find the book you need, and raise your hand to the shelf, to find it at once. You must know the library; you must have been a frequent visitor there; you must have learned how to use its card catalogues, and locate the sections where the books are placed which you need.

And you must familiarize yourself, also, with the Bible. I know it is hard. I know that the more you read the oftener you will be puzzled. But at least you can read the Gospels, and with a little help you can know something of the Epistles, and at small cost you can find study helps which will carry you into understanding of some of the great seed-thoughts which the Prophets gave to the world.

Jesus *lived by the Bible.* He quoted it in His temptation. He turned it upon His adversaries. He rediscovered its real meaning, and in His teaching made it live again. He found in it His trust in God as Father. Even as the Blessed Mother, when she sang Magnificat, reflected in her hymn the ancient

Song of Hannah, and gave it new meaning, so Jesus brought out of the Scriptures things old which He made new.

Again, you say, we have so little time. But the Ethiopian eunuch was treasurer of Queen Candice, a cabinet minister, so to speak, and in his busy life he found time to read—and found a Christian Evangelist to show him the meaning of what he was reading.

And, of course, Jesus died in trust and faith, because He *lived* in confidence of the Father's love. "The Son can do nothing of Himself," He said; "I live by the Father." He did not speak of Himself: "As I hear, I speak," He declared. When the men of influence in the nation turned against Him, and only simpler souls trusted Him, He "rejoiced in spirit, and said, I thank Thee, O Father, Lord of heaven and earth, that Thou hast hid these things from the wise and prudent, and hast revealed them unto babes; even so, Father, for so it seemed good in Thy sight."

Such trustful working in quiet harmony

with God characterized His life. Naturally, it showed forth in His death.

Learn, then, to live with Christ and to be like Him. Trust God more. Try to learn His will for you. Seek to find the treasures in His Word, even if you feel that they are overlaid with much dross. Do not rest satisfied with reading only the popular books of the day; read something about religion—and be careful in your selection of what you read. Pray. Pray for yourselves, and for the Church and its clergy. "A priest is either a great saint or a great sinner." He comes close to God, and in this nearness he may find the Father and reveal Him to you; or he may grow carelessly irreverent and learn that God is "a consuming fire." If you and I would die as Christ died—sure to the end—you and I must try to live as Christ lived.

I said that this final prayer of Jesus was the evening prayer of Jewish children. That night children in Jerusalem homes used it. And when Jesus, on the cross, prayed, "Father, into Thy hands I commend My spirit," it was a prayer that carried Him back to childhood days; it was as though He bowed His head, and folded His hands, and said: "Now I lay me down to sleep; I pray Thee, Lord, my soul to keep."

Long ago, you said the children's prayer. God grant that, as the shadows lengthen, and the evening comes, and the busy world is hushed, and the fever of life is over, and your work is done, you may have your child faith again. Then may God in His mercy grant you a safe lodging, and an holy rest, and peace at the last forever: through Jesus Christ our Lord.

PRINTED IN
THE UNITED STATES OF AMERICA
BY
MOREHOUSE PUBLISHING CO.
MILWAUKEE, WIS.